SPONTANEOUS DELUGE

BY:

ALICIA BUDHRAM

Editor: Sharp Editorial, LLC
Website: www.sharpeditorial.com

Publisher: Un-Filtered Publications
Website: www.unfilteredpublications.com

Cover design: Kevin Hansraj

Dedication

This book is dedicated to the dearest individuals who have been a monumental part of my journey, development, and growth. My love, gratitude, and highest regards.

Acknowledgments

Doll, 1,000,000 thank you's for your beautiful soul, understanding, and insights.

Anna, Laci, and Marla, I thank the universe for bringing us together.

Sometimes, in the depth of deep sleep, I hear the soft call of a heart. It pulls the frequency of mine, and I arise in haste, listening carefully. I hear nothing with my ears as you tug at the strings of my heart, playing strange notes I cannot decipher, yet I long to yield. Will you answer when I return your heart's call?

I have loved you in lifetimes before, temporarily forgetting you in the mad rush of life. It would be unthinkable for my heart to no longer recognize that rhythm... or those strange notes. Will you answer if I return your heart's call?

I crave your closeness, the fulfillment of long ago. It might seem like an ancient love story that you, in this lifetime, may not believe, but feeling you a thousand years apart feels like a nanosecond. I remember you, I do, but will you answer if I return your heart's call?

Will we bathe in the stars' lights? You will stand next to the moon, lighting my heart aflame. In your piercing dark gaze, I will drown my pains and lifetimes of shame.

You are just the same as when we met a thousand years ago.

Table of Contents

The Caterpillar

A cocoon of molten carcass,
Your end is a beginning.
You curl into your new life
Using the decaying process
As nutritive soup,
Slowly transforming.

Gather new cluster of cells,
Imagining a new reality.
Wings form inside shedding skin,
You work assiduously.

Creeping out in excitement
Beneath that fold,
Out morphs a butterfly,
A life with wings, behold!

Human

Royal, noble, and eminent,
Deemed highest among all species.
Over nature and all creatures, I rule.
I am, the one, heartily praised
For my brilliant mind and intellect;
I am, the one,
building skyscrapers and cities.

The greatest illusion, still, my body,
The falsity that I esteem to be real,
Oblivious that I am simply energy.
"Human, what have you become?"

I am a prisoner of my mind,
Locked and diseased.
Futile, I attempt to escape.
Suicidal, depression, and special needs,
All labels I fetch,
Thinking I must, somehow, be a huge mistake.

My mind is private, you say,
But you discern my thoughts through my actions;

The greatest folly, yet I see
The deformity of my own body,
Causing me to hate myself
In every conceivable way.

My IQ is the highest among generations past,
Yet my body has become broken and torn.
I no longer go outside to play.
Instead, I turn up the volume and plug in my headphones.

I seek friends from the virtual crowd,
Thousands of people I will never see or touch;
"My friends!" I say,
While I don't know my neighbor's name.
I am quite lonesome.
"Human, what have you become?"

Crippled and deformed
By my own limited thoughts,
Yet beautiful, supple, and firm,
My shell now slowly rots.
"Human, what have you become?"

Amnesia preys my mind;
I can't remember who I am.
I want to be everyone.
I want... I have... unlimited desires;

Restless, anxious, and agitated,
My own web I spun.

Contentment is illusive.
I have not a moment's peace.
I buy happiness, thinking it would last;
This chasm pulls me into depression.
I suffer inwardly where no one sees.

Thinking that mine
Is the smartest generation that ever lived,
I lock myself in my room and plug my ears;
I want to be left alone.
Socializing, my greatest fear.
I turned to myself and ask,
"Human, what have you become?"

I look at this civilized mess;
Nature weeps at my plunder.
Pillaging, greed, and discontentment,
Eventual devastation on the horizon;
I search for contentment, above and under.

Will you wake up now from thy illusory slumber?
It's time to follow your heart's lead;
This moment, right now,
You have but one chance to be a Hu-man being.

Dream

Wild flowers scattered on the ground;
The fountain birds splashed around.
Garden sprung forth in Earth's delight;
Dazed, she danced in delight.

Forest trails, an unfamiliar path.
A brush of grace she sought.
Birds chirped about happily;
From nature's mouth sprung melody.

Frogs croaked, bees buzzed louder;
Monkeys squealed at her sight.
Forest life blushed
As she spun and laughed in delight.

Naturally healing creatures
Rid those with pain and sorrows,
Spreading joy and hope
Of better, brighter tomorrows.

Artist

Each stroke of the brush is patient,
Slowly revealing a masterpiece.
Details carefully added
Before my release.

A pearl lies
In the depths of an oyster's shell.
Inside of my painting,
A thousand colorful strokes dwell.

Unraveling mysteries, an unending well;
I stare in awe
As if watching fireworks go off.
Struck, I was, by what I saw.

With the colors of my feelings,
I paint the world
After once shouting, "I possibly can't!"
Now the hues and shades emit
Like fissions of a radiation power plant.

I can create magic and magnificence
Or I can paint distortion and destruction;
I command my fingers,
"Feel not ever, restricted!"

The power to paint is now in my hands,
To strike murals with passionate messages
Or the darkness
My destructive mind envisages.

I did not recognize, and I did not see.
Oh, what a beauty I, myself,
Was carved out to be!

Now an image bubbles up
Deep inside of me;
I sit down to work,
Creating, unraveling another beauty.

Love's Colors

Is it light pink?
Is it navy blue?
Is it warm?
Is it tender?
Is it a scented white daisy?
Or a rose in its blood-red splendor?

Is it the color of kindness?
Does it flow like golden sand?
Can I paint it on a canvas?
Can it be bought?
Can it be sold?

Is it the color of compassion?
Is it a diamond ring?
Is it the color of an after-storm rainbow?
Or that of the first day of spring?

Passengers

Continuously, a train of thoughts
Run on the tracks of my mind;
Ever-changing scenes
Peek through the windows of my eyes.
Ceaselessly noisy passengers
Leave in haste,
Stamping their dirty footprints
In my private space.

Momentarily, I feel phobic from
The clutter of mud and dirt;
The track of my mind is polluted
With harmful past prints of hurt.

Dreams left unfulfilled,
Screaming for attention;
What choice did I have?
In this mad convention?
Choking my heart with resentment pain,
My ears couldn't stand the rustling passengers;
They sounded like rusty rain.

Thoughts screeching, metallically in haste,
Hounding my mind at very fast pace;
Dying to disembark at the next station,
Clearing my private space of all noisy creation.

Love

The most fabled among words –
Overused, misused, and abused;
Dancing on its stained originality,
Its value we've confused.

We've sold its innocence,
Desecrated its purity,
Poorly substituting its magnificence
with words –
Using lake to describe the sea.

Thinking that its potency relies on understanding
Is our biggest oversight yet;
That it is above rational thinking,
We never seem to get.

Love is beyond the elasticity of our minds,
Beyond being found.
It is way beyond comprehension,
Way more profound!

It is a volcanic explosion, burning walls of hate,
The coolness that gives courage to the weak,
The sweetness that warms hardened hearts,
And the healing we seek.

An overflowing river, it is,
A refreshing spring for tired souls,
An evergreen tree standing tall,
Not a reaction that another controls.

In every heart,
In every spirit that runs free,
Is love,

The light that burns eternally;
Infinitely.

Broken China

I came here to play.
It was fun at first.
I could never decide which was worse –
The fact that I fell down the fifth story,
Or the part when I kept wearily returning.

I shattered like fragile china,
tumbling off a rack.
Piece by piece, I was carefully glued back.
And although another fall was a guarantee,
I would never let that stop me.
I kept coming back to play again
And, eventually, became immune to the pain.

In the game of life, there is no reset.
I'm bad;
I'll never measure up to the standards they've set!
These unseen laws kept pushing me
Back to those hurting me.
Time had taken its toll.
My energy depleted;

I had left all my wounds untreated.

I could never be enough now, even if I tried,
But within the broken pieces, a faint voice cried,
"I am here. It was just a phase."
Forgotten in this endless maze
Is the life force that pulses every cell.
Broken was just my outer shell.

I have played through so many stages,
Cutting myself on my own sharp edges,
Now tired and alone,
Craving silence; craving home,
From this screaming unrest and painful game
That I don't want to ever play again.
Then maybe I'll have something more to share
Than poems about broken chinaware.

Fragrantly Gorgeous

Taking your minerals from a thorn
And perfuming the senses with
your essence,
I gaze at your soft, velvety petals,
utterly mesmerized!
Touching them gently,
I'm left awestruck.
My eyes fixed on the dew drops
Glistening like diamonds
under the morning sun.

You stand delicate, noble, and royal
In your thorny kingdom.
Your sweetness assails my senses;
Your fragrance spreads everywhere,
Never discriminating.
Such elementary elegance leaves me breathless.

Model

On the catwalk of life,
You are consistently modeling,
Angry, frustrated,
and constantly yelling.

See, the behavior I display
is modeled to me;
I observe.
I learn.
I practice.
I become, eventually.

Observing my friends and extended family,
My mom and my dad acting dysfunctionally;
Copying and pasting assiduously,
Being groomed by this reality,
It becomes the tendency.

The mind is private, you say,
But I observe your mind through your actions;
I model you in every way.

And as you model on the catwalk of life, consistently
I am modeling your behavior, unconsciously.
I then practice.
I learn.
I become, eventually.

Fear

Swirling waves dragged me deeper
Into the depths of its powerful crater.
Choking on intense fear,
Sensing instability, I drew near.
Not a single thought could I fathom,
But many they were, all random.

Fear rose, thundering in the head
From not knowing what lies ahead.
I shiver fearfully,
Scared of the nauseating uncertainty.

Everything conditioning,
Never spontaneity or whim;
Eyes looking upon an unfamiliar sight,
A barren golden desert, not a green in sight.

Frazzled and a bit dazed, somehow,
The frightened child
Trapped in the adult body asks,
"What now?"

Illusion

Love – the most elusive of all.
I thought I found it when I fell for you.
I was in love with my job,
My daughter when she was born;
Seeking and searching, I continued on.

I loved my new house,
My new car, my friends, and family.
When I am alone, why am I seeking, searching still?

Where is this fable that I am supposed to capture?
Hitting my head against the stone,
Now tired and alone,
I heard a faint whisper, "Look inside."
"Inside where?" I enquired.
"Inside of you."

But to my horror, I saw
Pitch black darkness, loneliness, hurt, and agony.
"Where is it?" I asked feebly.
The voice whispered, "Look further, still!"

I delved amidst the smelly muck,
Prodding and seeking.
Buried deep, barely a faint heartbeat
Is the whisper, "I am that which you seek."

Measurements

Desires meet the eyes.
Comparisons leave an anguished mind.
Measuring everything is a travesty;
Like someone else, I want to be.

Status measured in dollars,
Wealth acquired to prove worth,
Self-esteem trodden upon,
Contrasting looks of another sort.

Facial implants?
Surgical procedures?
I restructure the bones in my face
While the media sells my worth,
Consistently looking upon me with distaste.

Measuring my worth using another's cup,
My complexion makes me less;
"Lightening agents," I thought,
Help me look my best.

Worth measured by intelligence,
Am I a scholar?
Time and time again, comparing myself,
I felt smaller and smaller.

Others are better, perhaps;
I'm not as talented.
Battered and unsatisfied, I sink further;
Is measurement warranted?
Really, what is the guarantee?

Beauty Beyond

Is it possible for one
To be this beautiful
With petals silky smooth
And color, pink, my favorite?

Is it possible
To be stuck in muddy depths,
Yet standing tall,
Emerging unsoiled?

Is it possible that
The only way out is through,
To live in the murky waters
And rise above it?

Is it possible that
We can courageously rise
And bloom as beautifully
As the lotus does
From its muddy beginnings?

Religion

For the last 2,500 years, you swept across the globe,
A microbe infiltrating the psyche,
Tearing humankind to shreds.
Believing in an authority –
Monarchical, patriarchal, hierarchical –
We've become blindfolded warheads.

Preaching love while living in disunity,
Destroying the basis of our community.
Instilling archaic beliefs inclined,
Never envisioned I could be refined.
"Savior said!" said the majority.
"Who am I to question authority?"
Discriminatory and insinuating,
Dualistic propensities.

Righteous vs. sinner;
Right vs. wrong;
Angel vs. devil;
You vs. me;
They vs. us;

We are better;
They are doomed.
Divisive and discriminatory;
Man-made, most definitely!

Identity In Crisis

When I entered your family,
You taught me,
"You're a boy!"
"You're a girl!"
And you created my first identity.
You gave me a name;
I believed it to be me
My second identity.
You taught me to pray,
And you told me, "This is your religion!"
My next identity.

And so never really far was I
From my next identity.
My personality developed.
Emotional patterns formed.
Identifying with everything,
Identifying with everyone,
And believing that I was
All that was taught to me.

I was never allowed
To simply exist
As a piece of life.
Everyone wanted
To teach me something.
I had to blend in with the crowd.

Curled up, I was
In my cold, hard shell.
As time passed by,
No longer could I tell
What was me and what was not.
Lost was I, taking on identities
And only living the life I was taught.

Never allowed was I to simply be.
My identities, my acts,
My roles, my labels,
I made them me.
I fought;
I rebelled;
I cried;
I tortured;
I died;
I put to death
The false identities

I took to be me.

But, look at me now.
Oh, what have I become?
A twisted, deformed,
Unrecognizable me.
I, the one in whom all potentiality, creativity, and spontaneity
exists

I have become a catastrophe,
Because I was never allowed
To simply be.

Beliefs

Beliefs – the age-old and new-age disease,
Viral over the human race.
We believe we've come to know it all,
Yet fulfilment remains, an endless chase.

We are conditioned to perceive the world
As we currently do.
The more convinced we are, the fiercer we defend
What we think we are, what belongs to us,
And what we believe to be true.

Today, we fight and support wars,
All in the name of beliefs;
We raise our children with emotional scars,
All for our beliefs.
Against the innocent, we commit endless evils,
Throwing around hateful speech like a thousand needles,
All for our beliefs.
We remain quiet while others are plundered and killed,
Watch without compassion as their blood is spilled,
Yet "justice!" is what we demand for ourselves,

All for our beliefs.

Beliefs – a natural disaster, sparing nothing in its path,
Leaving us divided in its disastrous aftermath.

Our love is conditional and only shown
To those who believe the things we do.
What have we done in the name of belief?
What has it turned us into?

The One

Look toward the golden sun.
Have you any clue
That the one seeing its radiance
Is the one that's really you?
You – the unique and potential-packed;
How far you've strayed off track!
To explain this, I could write on and on;
That you, ENERGY, you're the one!

The one who splits thoughts apart;
The one who beats the heart;
The one who speaks through your mouth;
The one who looks about;
The force that pulses 100-trillion cells;
The one who reads and spells;
The one whose life forces keeps the body functional;
The one who is not a no-body;
The one who uses the mind;
The one so exquisitely designed;
You, ENERGY.
Yes, you're that one!

Duality

You split everything in your path;
Evolution has felt the brunt
of your cruelty.
Opposites are the main course;
Comparison, the entrée.

You served a dessert of dependency,
Ruled by intellectuality,
Bisecting and dissecting every specialty.

You have split the impossible, the atom.
Your ego separates from self;
Master follows servant instead;
More damages we are unable to fathom.

Isn't it time you decide you've had enough?
Your climb, upward,
Formative,
Determined to be one - the only alternative.

Scientists

Evidences must be adequate;
Billowing towers of Dubai you create.

Rocket science, a successful history,
Yet who you are, remains a mystery.

You explain how dunes turned into land,
But your existence is what you fail to understand.

You fly in a spaceship you constructed
While you are unable to unravel the mysteries
Surrounding your stories.

You can split an atom into subatomic particles;
News riles with horrific articles.

But your greatness lies in silence,
Not in your technological brilliance.
Now it's time for the internal science
Of your eternal eminence.

Slave Of My Mind

Cold, afraid, and alone,
I lay still and almost dead.
Drowning in thoughts,
There's so much left unsaid.

With fear and desperation seeping in;
Darkness is already within.

Determined not to break,
A few deep breaths I take.
Breathless, climbing uphill,
Desperate to just sit still.

The sun hiding its kindly light,
Not a ray of hope in sight.
In the dark, cold room
Of my distraught mind
Remains I, the soul, confined.

Wounded

Enmeshed in matter,
Watching my fond dreams shatter,
I became entangled,
Bewildered, and mangled.

Daily struggles I met.
I became an awful wreck.
I searched, I begged, and I took the blame;
I complained.
I screamed a name.

Life became somewhat of a hell.
So, I stayed curled up underneath my shell.
Running around, sometimes out of breath,
In the wheel of life and death.

Lost and battered,
A hundred pieces scattered;
Wounded, I fell
Down the bottomless pit of a well.

Architect Of Destiny

I laid the foundation,
One building block at a time,
Sands that hold the secrets of time.

An empire that withstood
thousands of years –
Stories seep through the cracks;
Open your ears.

In Earth's bosom,
Shielded by the stars' light
Rested molecules of breath,
Creatures of the night.

Waters carrying secrets of centuries unknown,
and the sun witnessing all the drama silently shown.

The moon flashes pictures of flowing events,
And planets dance at space and time events.

Silently witnessing the human plight,
Searching for the light, thousands' die in trite.
I arise from sleep and get on the flight.
Humanity, it's your right.

Death

I stand on the precipice of despair.
I think to myself, "I hate to be here."
Stormy thoughts, a whirlwind raging through my head,
"What would it be like if I were dead instead?"
Tumultuous thoughts, emotions in a heap;
For now, I will have to count and hope to fall asleep.

Death is my friend, my sweet reprieve.
I packed my bags. I'm ready to leave.
You will take me on a journey of silence;
Erase my pain; wipe my existence.
I can almost feel you approaching near;
Many endless, meaningless words here.

I've had enough caffeine and blood-red ink;
I'm giving up now. I'm on the brink.
Hide me, dear death, in your snug, little nest.
All they have said about you is illusory;
I know you; you will bring me rest.

Toxicity

Poisonous, cloistered claustrophobia
Squeezing my life energies;
Weaker I become with each drop of venom.
Every single word, a poisonous bite
Aimed to instill fear,
Thrusting me into flight,
Crushing the life of a newborn dream.

Hatred and resentment
You spilled.
Nauseating, nervous tension;
Little did you know,
I was waiting; I was still.

Injecting the antidotes of self-love
Was a block to your horrible influence;
Enough of your poisonous substance, dear.
Self-love is my insurgence;
T'was a time for my resurgence.

Passion

A consuming fire envelopes the heart,
An erupting volcano, like a firework,
Emitting golden sparks.

An avalanche of feelings is
Cracking my veritable shield.
I'm being swept away
By raging winds of thoughts.
Sitting here, tensed,
My stomach tied in knots.

Should I trust my fiery heart
Or should I skip this part?
On the edge of the cliff, longing,
Contemplating jumping.

Storms of whistling emotions
Spinning in a tornado solution,
Flung into cyberspace.
Reprieve I taste.

Upon the doors of my heart
Hung stars of burning passions.
The heart knows no vigilance;
Save me now before I
Sink into rapturous indulgence.

Nature's Embrace

In this dying, decaying carcass,
I took a second birth,
Resurrecting from the ashes
Of death's inferno.
Pain became my nutritive soup.
In death, I was alone.

The darkness was beautiful;
I could hide here, and no one would notice
That I've been missing for eons.
But here, my fears barraged me daily.
Shadows hauntingly trailed me,
Yet I liked it; it kept me safe.

Light burned my eyes and exposed my wounds.
"No!" shouted the skies. "I will heal your wounds!"
Turn your face towards the sun.
Let it melt your dark, cold heart.
Let the fiery heat cleanse your pain
And the raging sea wash away your fears.
Let the Earth's gravity pull you

From the bowels of wreckage;
Nature's womb –
Let it be where you rest your head.
And the wind –
It will take you into its cool embrace
And breathe you back to life.

Guide

Each week, you pushed me further.
I was vulnerable, broken, and afraid.
Whenever I needed someone,
You willingly rushed to my aid.

You saw potential when all I saw
Was a lump of useless clay.
Not a lot of people believed in me.
The gravel in their voices kept me at bay.

You nudged me back to who I forgot I was
And glued me together with motherly love.
Working tirelessly, I built a new foundation.
The conditioned me, I slowly got rid of.

With wisdom and outstretched arms,
You gently calmed every fear.
You gathered the shattered remnants
With kindness, understanding, and care.

When I screamed, you soothed my pain;

You fed my self-esteem
And had me back on my feet again.
Tenderly, you unraveled my unconscious mystery.
I finally made peace with my history,
And I was brought back from the brink of unreality
With your guidance and skill of self-mastery.

Rising

I was planted in the forest of the past.
Memories of hurt and shame,
My fertilizers, I knew by name.

Months passed, waiting for a shot.
You were patient, kept watering the seed daily,
Imagining a root.

The fern spread quickly
Across the forest floor
Whilst I sat there all alone.

Waiting seemed endless to you
Whilst I was still;
No visible shot.
Those moments of silence gave me power,
Sustaining and encouraging my pursuit.

After what seemed like eons,
I finally gave a shot;
See, it won't be long before

I celebrate my first fruit.

I rose like a billowing tower in the sky;
I grew into an evergreen tree!
The time I was stuck was quietly spent
Spreading the roots I needed to sustain me.

Solitary Confinement

Confined to this wall of flesh,
Alone with my shadowy thoughts,
My mind has imprisoned me.

Cold and solitary,
The mind's wall, damp and gloomy,
Light-headed, I sink into the void.
"Why is it so dark in here?"
Screams my inner child.

Surreal, I'm walking through life.
My mind, a mirage; a barren dessert.
A fallen victim I am to these imaginings.
Questioning why it has to be me,
I pray for an oasis, a drop of alchemy.

Will I ever feel the sunshine in my hair
And hear the birds singing sweet songs?
The light – will I ever stop being afraid of it?
Will I ever breathe the fresh, salty air?

Will I ever open my intuitive eyes
And leave this place of confinement
Inside my body?

Edge Of Abyss

Pain echoing, faintly still,
Ringing from the slap on my cheek;
I stood there, cold and chilled,
Somehow afraid to speak.

My inner voice raised in defiance.
His fist raised in ignorance.
Forgive him, I quickly did,
But the pain lingered
From what he said and did.

I allowed it continually,
Had not established boundaries,
But on the edge of darkness,
Shrouded in the veil of insecurity,
I finally understood;
I wasn't his property.

Standing tall and menacing,
I looked him in the eye,
Realizing his actions were

Like a petulant child.
I screamed, "NO!
I'm a human being, you know!"
I drew the line;
His hands slowly declined.
I stood my ground.
He retreated.
Finally, I breathed a sigh of relief.

Introversion

The salient moon was high in the sky.
'Twas was a peaceful sight,
Peeking through the clouds,
Drenching me in her pale moonlight.

I contemplate chasms of emotions,
Allowing the warmth of the breeze
To ease the turbulence in my mind
And soothe my dis-ease.

The sand trickling through my fingers,
Crashing waves and a pulsating heartbeat.
Deeply, I inhale,
Faintly breathing out sighs of relief.

Attached to the past
is my inquisitive mind.
"Do I have a purpose?
Are there more of my kind?"

The silent introspection

Finally leads to a decision –
I must follow my heart;
Giving love is my only part.

Origin

Genesis, beginning, inception,
Point, dot, seed, and a zero allusion,
Denoting origins,
The potential to expand into more.

A seed springing forth a tree,
Graphs and pencils, a compass pointing north,
The potential power of a dot-like atom
Creating nuclear emissions,
Zeroes adding to create gazillions,
Light waves from the sun pointing to Earth.

Thou art light –
A universal actuality
With unlimited potential to expand;
A possible cosmic quality.

Genesis, beginning, inception,
Point, dot, seed, and a zero allusion;
The beginning holds secrets untold.
Stories are many; mysteries, they hold.

Am I?

Am I nothing?
Am I intrinsically infinite?
Am I eternal?
Am I collapsible?

Am I frissons of light?
Am I a spark?
Am I intangible?

Am I stardust?
Am I energy?
Am I consciousness?
Am I imperishable?

Am I destined for greatness
Or should I contend with my lot?
Surely, there must be more to me
Than what I have been taught.

It's in my core
That I am something more.

Earth's Destruction

Earth slowly and silently weeps;
Destroying it and its precious inhabitants,
Is civilization taking great leaps?

Religious dogma runs at a fast pace;
Hating and killing,
Conquering and dividing the human race.

Economic developments, a cataclysmic chase.
Mutations and modifications,
Changing DNA, changing every face.

Scientists resolve to find a solution,
Ironically using the other hand
To speed up dissolution.

High in demands are
Chemical warfare and radiation plants
Whilst we ignore sea life, the birds, and the ants.

Political dominance cripples the masses.

The people are misled;
They look on with rainbow glasses.

Deforestation, economic viability;
Business men filling their pockets,
Normalizing disloyalty.

Plastic, a nonsensical calamity
Conditioned by materiality;
Humans have forgotten their reality.

Each, a life insurance policy;
Who does not understand universal brotherhood
And co-dependency?

False Power

The voice is menacing and filled with hate,
Spilling lies, denial and distaste,
Accusing and foisting horrible words;
The mind is left in a confusing state.

Her actions trigger his fear-based recesses;
He's afraid of her successes.

She cowers in fear; her heart bleeds;
She's done being a defender of his misdeeds.

She raises her head in defiance
And walks away without a backward glance.

Moonlight Affair

Lying naked on the beach at night,
Clothed only in the pale moonlight.
Winds of desires whip thy face;
Warm sand touches thy skin,
gently, with no haste.

Lips moistened by the wind
Leaving its salty aftertaste.
Musical waves crash against the banks,
Splashing notes across thy face.

Venus trembles in her glory and might;
It was a love affair, the moon and her,
Kissing every area with her full moonlight,
Missing nothing in her sight.

Flames spark in her feminine heart;
She revels in the sensation.
The scent of the ocean perfuming her senses;
Engulfed, she was, in ecstasy.

Cosmic Flight

I landed on the stars
After my cosmic flight.
Ethereal and sparkling
Were the guardians of light.

Beings that floated from left to right,
Whispering a question, "Are you a passenger?
A mission of earthly might?"

Glimmer reflected by tranquility's mirror,
Jolting a memory of this familiar sight –
A flicker of crystalized shimmer.
Gracefully poised under the threshold of light,
This world of light is an intimate sight.

Frissons of stardust fell, engulfing me;
Cosmic connection, a mission of might.
Orange hues pulling me close
Into the bosom of light,
Melting my past under the sun's delight.

I opened up to serenity's light;
Tranquil angels of the night.

Intricate Web

Patterns, propensities,
Conditioning, latent tendencies;
Where are these recorded in me?

My thoughts are counted by sparks.
The picture firing within me,
Observed and witnessed by technology.
Can they really see me?

But who is the 'I" that claims me?
Where are my memories and programs stored?
Is it in my physicality
Rooted in my psyche?

What is this entity
Who feels every experience?
Why do I long to be me?
To taste my highest potentiality?

Mysterious Mind

Fascinating, intricate mystery;
Practical, logical, prudent,
A thought facility.

You devise, you calculate,
You reason, and you create.

Thinkaholicism, your plight;
You nudge the body to fight or flight.
Fear-based, an ever-present attorney
Defending the case, need to be right.

Mind, you behave like a petulant child –
Automatic, dualistic, and thinking fast,
Keeping me buried deep in the past.

Filled with resentment and shame,
I refuse insanity's name.

You are my thought facility,
Not my identity.
I am the master;
You are the tool for creativity.

Almighty Dollar

Its magnetism rivals the moon.
Greed and despair creates the mood
For something so often,
So fervently pursued.
We steal, cheat, kill, destroy, and torture,
All for the almighty dollar.

The most attractive physicality,
Dragging minds into calamity,
Pulling humans enslaved in a predicament
And those seeking security.
Wearing the body thin,
Hanging men like puppets on a string.

Almighty dollars of greatest significance,
Capturing the mind with arrogance;
Domination with defiance syndicate,
Worshipped as the God of our time.
The dollar, the almighty;
Present-day reality.

Pioneer

Resourceful, creative,
Artistic, eloquent, and intelligent,
Your natural abilities;
Dependency, attachment, doubts, despair –
Illusory lies or adaptive tendencies?

Expander, discoverer, adventurer –
Your natural abilities;
Fear, anger, dislike, and resentment –
Veils of illusion or acquired tendencies?

Ingenious, inventive, imaginative –
Your natural abilities;
Blame, shame, and the victim game –
Illusory egoic games or acquired tendencies?

Strength, courage, will-power,
Valorous, and valiant –
Your natural qualities;
You are an instrument of
Conscious potential capacity.

Stardust

Celestial and glorious, once I was;
Divinity, my very form;
An exploding star with not a clue;
Eminence, radiance, a stardust storm.

Atoms from countless different stars,
Billions of years ago,
Are now a part of me;
My eyes, my face, a starlight glow.

The stardust, a flicker, faded
Into barely a glimmer;
Washing with love, a continuous process.
Daily, I sat in the stillness.
Inward pointed the compass,
And will lead you upward, not in the mass.

Recognition dawned slowly;
I remembered my nobility,
My sovereignty, and my mastery.
There I was, gently guided
By a spark back home to me.

Childhood

Together, we grew up, running about,
Eating from the same plate,
Watching sunsets, hugging each other,
Sharing stories, watching cartoons, and
Pledging to be friends forever.

Long hours we played, we talked, and
We shared our fears;
Laughter bubbled from our hearts,
Ringing like music to our ears.

Through our lenses, we saw not a difference;
A lot of empathy and a ton of resilience.

Thirty years down the road
They started a code –
Racism, color, and discrimination,
Conditioned by differences,
A new fixation.
Programmed with labels, we were branded like jeans;
We modeled it, breaking up our teams.

They built gaps in small inconceivable snaps;
It is sad how our story ends
With us forgetting, we were childhood friends.

Depression

Curled up in a melancholic ball,
Vertigo, falling into nothingness.
Thoughts screaming endlessly in my mind,
Sinking further into the depths of sorrow.
Darkness hugs me closer to its gloom.
I want light, but I'm afraid of its trite.
Claustrophobic squeals tighten my throat;
Light-headed, I sink into void.
Despondency is I knew.
I wish to breathe life, but I feel so alone.
Hopelessness and despair are my throne.
Daily, I sat waiting by the phone,
Hoping you'd call to check if I'm home.
Lonely, feeling scared to the bone,
Rambling monsters constantly beating
Drums of raging pessimism in my head.
Sadness and loss stoke my life
Please, please, I'm tired; leave me be.
I want to sink into deep sleep.
Reprieve from these monsters, I seek
Peace and silence only, I desire!

Beloved

I gaze at you in wonder,
Amazed by your shining, glimmering beauty.
You're light, sparkling magnificence.
You held me when I shake;
You told me I am no fake;
You praised me when I lost my esteem;
Patiently, raising my worth,
my value redeemed.

You showed me the beauty I hid within;
You always knew I'd win.
Consistently, without fail,
You stood waiting, every day,
To wrap me in your coat of love.
Now, I look at the universe with love;
I smile and say, "I knew it was you all along."
My dearest beloved.

Love Making Vs Sex

Misconstrued, confused
Shifting the human psyche
An art, perhaps? A sales package? Captivity?
Possessing, domineering, abashed -
An overcast
Deceit, cheat, blame, shame
How could this last?

Relationships – rocky
Promoting illusions
Displayed in expectations gallery
Galling, Comparing sex as love
Atrocious, if not ridiculous

Fixated on this pleasure-seeking diversity
On an endless search to satisfy the chasm
Sucked into to the quicksand of a vacuum
Not a single clarity
Making love - in a competition
With sex - a crazy obsession
Sex, world dominance gained
Victory over love – an art no longer sustained

Home

Majestic and glorious I was once
Trudged the path of entropy, certainly
Divinity was my very name
Now I hide in the shame
I am tired of the game
Inward pointed the compass
Will lead you upward not in the mass
It was dark at first
The star dusts a flicker, a glimmer
Washing with love, a continuous process
Daily I sat in silence
In the stillness, I progressed
Slowly remembered my nobility, my sovereignty
Guided by a star back home

www.ingramcontent.com/pod-product-compliance
Lightning Source LLC
LaVergne TN
LVHW041206080426
835508LV00008B/824